FRAMES

Visit our website
readframes.com

Contact us
hello@readframes.com

Advertise with us
advertise@readframes.com

Submit your work
submit@readframes.com

Subscribe
readframes.com/join

Follow us
instagram.com/frames_magazine
facebook.com/framesmagazine
youtube.com/framesmagazine

Receive the newsletter
readframes.com/framesletter

Listen to the podcast
readframes.com/podcast

Editor-in-Chief
Tomasz Trzebiatowski

**Reviews, Interviews
and Podcasts**
W. Scott Olsen

Copy Editor
Emily Ihde

Layout and Design
Dani Corbett

Social Media Assistant
Nayoung Yoon

Cover photo
John Paul Caponigro

Contributors
John Paul Caponigro
Gary Beeber
Filip Wolak
Ray Harris
Kasra Karimi
Lynne Blount

Conversations
Donald Miralle
Maxx Wolfson

FRAMES Vol. 7 April 2022
ISSN 2673-5393

FRAMES is a quarterly publication. The
content published in the magazine reflects
the opinions of the respective contributors,
and do not always represent the views of
the publishers and editorial team.

Printed in the United Kingdom at Taylor
Brothers (Bristol) Ltd, on EMAS certified
uncoated paper.

Times are difficult, challenging, troubling… I am looking for adjectives, but none seem adequate to describe the severity of the current situation. Where does photography fit into it all? Does it have its place? Does it even matter?

The more I think about it, the more I am convinced that there is important energy in every single artistic act being performed on this Earth these days, wherever it might be. And it is this combined energy from us all, as individual artists small and large (photographers, musicians, sculptors, singers, writers…), that will withstand the evils of this world, that will keep the world on track and not allow it to lose its dignity and most important values.

Yours truly,

Tomasz Trzebiatowski
Editor-in-chief, FRAMES Magazine

tomasz@readframes.com

VOLUME 7

Contents

MY ANTARCTICA

John Paul Caponigro

First Awareness, First Approach

I became aware of Antarctica when I was a boy and my mother designed Eliot Porter's book. I marveled at the octogenarian who launched into such a great adventure so late in life. His images suggested that he had gone to another planet without leaving the earth. I made one of those deep silent wishes that often seal our fate; I wanted to go. Twenty years later, I made my first voyage. Having traveled to the tip of South America, we sailed across the circumpolar current through the dread Drake Passage, the roughest waters in the world. So rough that we often couldn't walk much less in a straight line and had to wedge ourselves into our bunks to catch what little sleep we could. After two days, the water calmed and on the far horizon, we saw a glimpse of what looked like a tiny block of ice that after hours of approach turned out to be much larger than a city block. We couldn't see where it came from and could only imagine where it was going.

land can't be seen here
ice floats before on beyond
horizons obscured

Antarctica CXCII
John Paul Caponigro
Black Head, 2014

Enchanted By Ice

I was unprepared to be enchanted by ice. Time and time again
we came across gardens of sculpted ice. Floating around, into,
and through them, every angle presented a different set of
possibilities. Greek columns changed into boats, boats into
dragons, dragons into goddesses. Sometimes we'd see the
same iceberg days later and we could barely recognize it. Their
chameleonic cascades border on the hallucinatory and move
so fast you have to be fully present or you'll miss a once-in-a-
lifetime opportunity that can never be repeated. Icebergs only
present ten percent of themselves, the rest they keep hidden
underwater. Ice bobs, melts, rains, cracks, tilts, tips, rolls over,
sometimes explosively. We learned to read the ice to know how
to approach it and when to leave, not unlike dealing with a wild
animal. Always changing, in a perpetual state of motion, neither
a liquid nor a solid, ice feels like a living thing.

deep waters cold creep
abyss bottoms endless nights
changing days on land

Antarctica CCLVIII
John Paul Caponigro
Pleneau Bay, 2018

Wild Weather

The weather in Antarctica expresses every mood. The seas can be so
rough you can't stand. The winds may be so fierce they'll blow you
down. Ice will fly sideways through the air. Waterfalls blow back up the
mountains they descend from. And then everything gets impossibly calm
and the waters become glassy mirrors. Fog may roll in leaving you to see
only dim shadows, bringing yet another form of disorientation. But the
whitest days are the ones without a cloud in the sky when the sun blazes
down and back again from the ice in a blinding heat that makes you feel
transparent. While much of Antarctica feels untouchable, it penetrates
you in every way.

hot summer's exhale
sea ice retracts then expands
cold winter's inhale

Antarctica CLXXI
John Paul Caponigro
Lemaire Channel, 2018

Sometimes The Sun Doesn't Rise, Sometimes The Sun Doesn't Set

Time moves differently in Antarctica, more so the further south you go. On our
first voyage, we sailed into the most magnificent sunset I've ever experienced.
As we were sailing through the high peaks of the Lamaire Channel, the sky
caught fire, full of golds and corals and lavenders, rapidly reflected in the water.
Being photographers we rushed to make as many exposures as we could before
it faded, but our cards quickly filled. We rushed into our cabins to download
our images and return as fast as we could. And we began shooting again. Again
we filled our cards in disbelief that the fire was still there. We repeated our
ritual. On the third round we began to slow down, overwhelmed in amazement
that the fire showed no sign of fading. It lasted hours. At the right time in the
right place the sun never sets. We still have a hard time believing that it wasn't a
dream. But we have the photographs to prove it.

the sun does not set
whole seasons of day and night
the sun does not rise

Antarctica CXXX
John Paul Caponigro
Half Moon Island, 2011

Understanding Antarctica

There are things about Antarctica that you cannot see and
can only hear or read about. The largest body of fresh water
on earth is frozen Antarctica. It contains 90% of all ice on
earth. There are lakes inside the ice cap that are larger than
America's Great Lakes. Built up over 40 million years, the
icecap is so massive it pushes the continental crust down
one and a half miles below sea level. There are many south
poles; geographic, magnetic, geomagnetic, ceremonial and
more. Days and nights can last months. It has never had
an indigenous culture. Individually, these facts amaze –
combined, they overwhelm. And Antarctica silently waits
for us to catch up and discover even more.

dry valleys shelter
one million years without snow
spread crystal deserts

Antarctica XL
John Paul Caponigro
Neko Harbor, 2007

Conservation Works

Antarctica is prophetic. The most pristine continent bar none, Antarctica is not a nation itself but rather an International Territory devoted to science. It offers many examples of how conservation works. Whaling is just one of its many success stories. In the twentieth century alone nearly 3 million cetaceans were wiped out, in what may have been the largest cull of any wild animal – in terms of total biomass – in human history. That practice has been stopped (largely) and many populations are springing back. Every year, more and more Humpback whales return to the area. It's been a joy to witness. We've seen them shortly after birth and long after death. We've seen them leap in the air and play with us, looking us in the eye at arm's length. The slow shrinking of the ozone hole after the cessation of using CFS is another great success story. There are many examples of how conservation works, sometimes more quickly than anticipated. Climate is changing and so Antarctica's ice is melting and this, in turn, is beginning to change global ocean currents, weather, and sea level. Will we work together to protect not just Antarctica but also us?

here weather changes
climate crises everywhere
butterfly wings flap

Antarctica CVIII
John Paul Caponigro
Neumayer Channel, 2008

Images May Fail, Words May Fail

Antarctica tests our limits and so expands us. It's illuminating to understand that images have limits (some things can't be photographed) and words have other limits (some things can't be put into words), yet the synergy struck between words and images can bring even more to light. It's not just the absence of other senses – sound, scent, touch and how they also activate mind, heart, and gut; as much as we capture and share, briefly holding still our moving world, there is always more mystery to explore. Art can be a way if not of transcending our limits then entering more fully into them and being filled to overflowing.

torn paper mountains
words images not enough
oceans of first drafts

Antarctica CCXXII
John Paul Caponigro
Danco Island, 2017

JOHN PAUL CAPONIGRO

John Paul Caponigro is an internationally collected visual artist and
writer who leads unique adventures in the wildest places on earth to
help people creatively make deeper connections with nature.

He dreamed of going to Antarctica as a child and began his
physical voyages as a young man. His obsession with this other
world within our world has compelled him to make varied
responses, creating different kinds of images (straight and altered)
and different kinds of writing (prose and poetry). In this piece,
Caponigro uses the Japanese form haibun (combining prose and
haiku) to touch the sublime nature of his subject.

www.johnpaulcaponigro.com

PERSONALITIES

2017-2022

Gary Beeber

I first met Jimmy Mack at
the Polar Bear Plunge in
Southampton, NY where he was
dressed as a mermaid. In this
photograph, he's posing for me in
his pool in Southampton, NY.

Jimmy on a float
Gary Beeber
Southampton, New York

Emily is an artist who's art form is her hair, makeup and clothing. Her hair changes every month, which led me to make a documentary film about her called "Emily's Do."

She says: "Self expression is my motivation, I like for people to see what's on the inside, on the outside."

I first met Emily at a friend's art opening in Dayton, Ohio. She had multicolored hair that was cut into shapes, and was wearing a white faux fur coat with bananas printed all over it. I knew right away that I wanted to photograph her, so I did what I always do; introduced myself and gave her my card. I told her to check out my website and if she liked my work to give me a call, which she did. We met for coffee and talked about taking her picture. The first photo session turned into many sessions and eventually led to making the film.

Emily Smoking
Gary Beeber
Dayton, Ohio, 2020

This gentleman is a New York City
night-life personality, which means that
he makes his living by dressing up and
appearing/hosting at late night parties
and venues throughout New York City.
In this photograph, he's posing in a tiny
room in the Theater District.

Black Feather
Gary Beeber
New York City, 2017

Steven D. is a very patriotic American
from Long Island, NY. In this picture
he is posing for me in a suburban
setting in Sag Harbor, NY.

Steven D., God Bless America!
Gary Beeber
Sag Harbor, New York, 2017

Scott Baker is a legendary geek performer, master of the bally stage at Coney Island, actor, magician, writer and cancer survivor.

I first met Scott at the Coney Island Circus Sideshow where he was performing as the outside talker. An outside talker (popularly known as a barker) stands outside a sideshow and gets people to pay admission by his banter and by performing geek acts such as hammering a solid steel nail or screwdriver up his nose.

For many years Mr. Baker was also Santa Claus at Bloomingdale's in Manhattan.

Although I spent a lot of time with Scott (I produced a documentary film about him called "BALLY-MASTER"), I don't feel like I ever really knew him.

Scotty in his living room, NYC
Gary Beeber
New York City, 2017

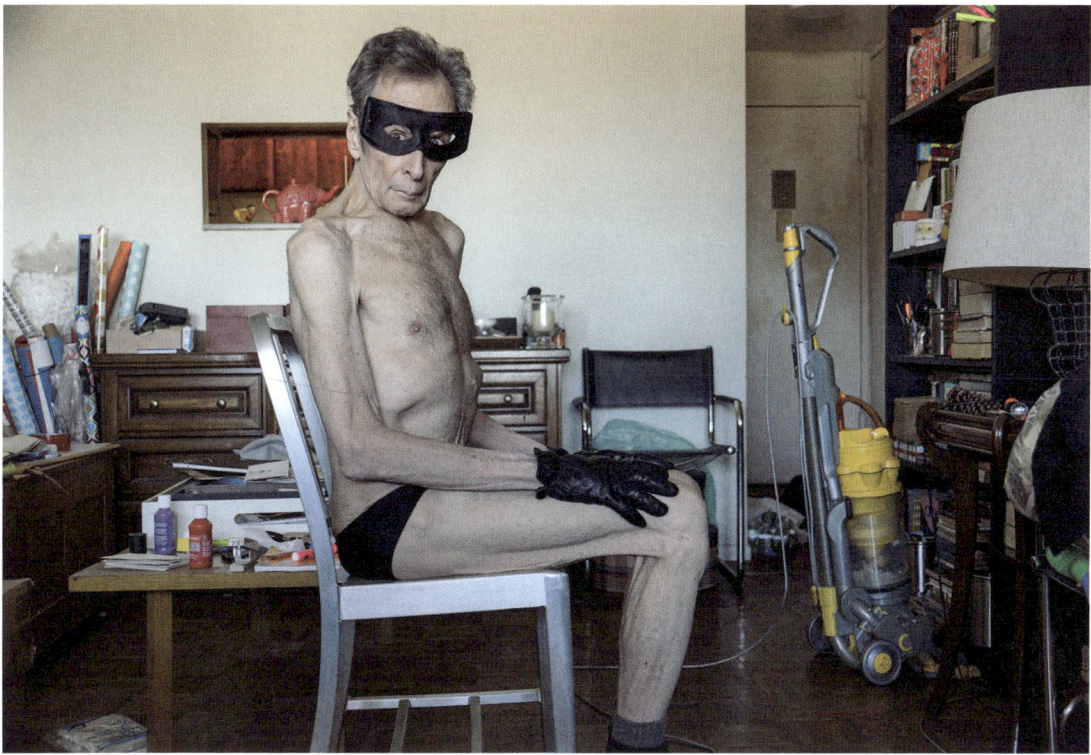

David Slater is an artist who lived in
Sag Harbor, NY, at the time I shot this
portrait. He is a painter, but might be
best known for his eccentric collage
work. His whole apartment was made
into a collage, as well as his car.

Artist in his car (David Slater)
Gary Beeber
Sag Harbor, New York, 2017

Bettina May is an international burlesque star whom I had the pleasure of working with many times when I produced the Off-Broadway Show, "Gotham Burlesque." In this picture she's posing for me in her bedroom in the apartment she lived in at the time in Brooklyn.

Burlesque Star in her bedroom
Gary Beeber
Brooklyn, New York, 2017

GARY BEEBER

Gary Beeber is an award-winning American
photographer/filmmaker who has exhibited in
galleries and museums throughout the United
States and Europe.

www.garybeeber.com

WINTER FROM ABOVE

Filip Wolak

There's not much flying during the winter. The days are short, it's cold, and you have to clean the snow off your airplane every time it snows, regardless of if you go flying or not. And, when all is said and done, the engine is reluctant to start!

As Lady Winter settles in during the first weeks of the new year, the days start to get longer and weather becomes more predictable; the season becomes an absolute joy for aviation. Never mind those huge swings of temperature though! With the air being more stable, the airplane zips along effortlessly with almost double the power (dense and cold air is good for the engine and wings). I am also a bit more "seasoned" against the elements – the cold doesn't bother me as much anymore. And it gets really, really cold up there!

Joint Flight
Filip Wolak
Westchester, New York State, 2016

After all, what difference does a slight discomfort make when faced with stunning wintry views. Fresh fallen snow is like a blank canvas, on which the sun paints amazing geometric figures by its light and shadow. Everything is covered with a pristine white blanket – no visual distractions, only a pure, minimal form. The outlines of real objects shift into the area of abstraction – some of them invoke curiosity, some of them tend to surprise at the discovery of what they actually represent. I have always been fascinated by monochromatic nature or winter – in the air and on the ground alike – everything is dormant, peaceful, almost surreal in its absolute stillness.

Flying in itself is a form of meditation, and my solitude is deliberate, not a randomness of the moment. Only being in this state is it possible to get close to nature and open yourself enough to notice the revelations of her visual secrets to you. The mind becomes sharp and focused while I look with my heart rather than with my mind. Being mentally comfortable and rested is key, as everything is in constant motion, you need to pay constant attention to whatever surrounds you. It is a blessing and a curse – an ever changing environment always offers a fresh view, but the moments last only a split second.

Red Roof
Filip Wolak
Eastern Pennsylvania, 2016

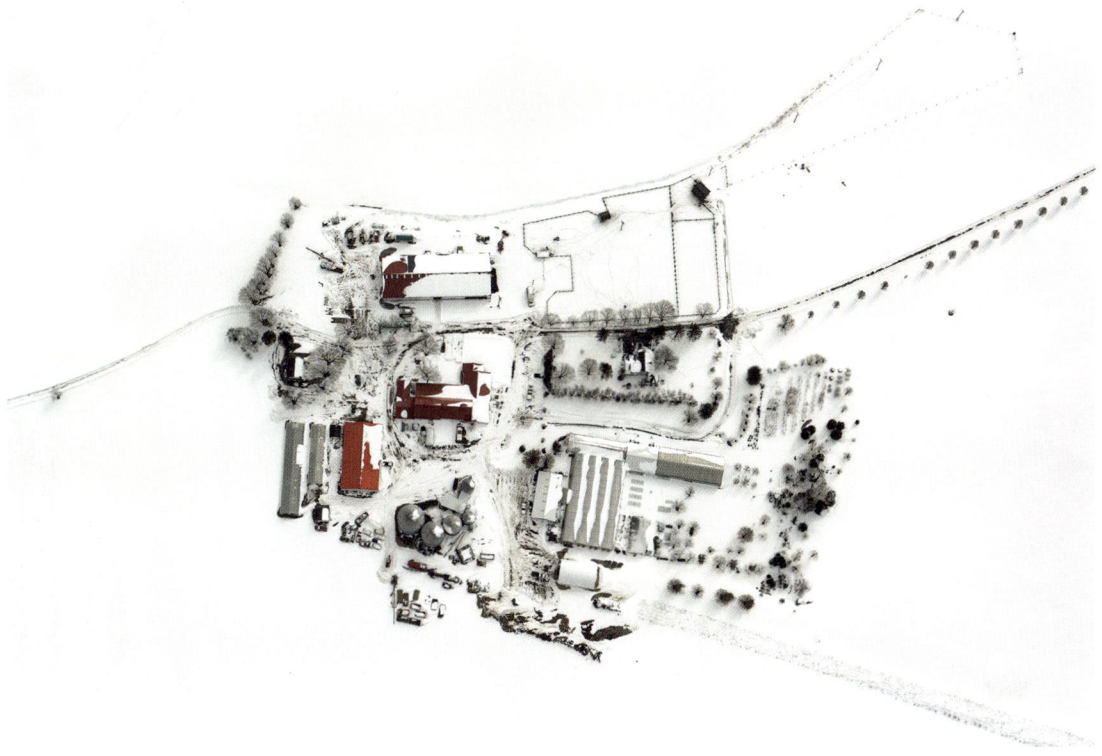

Being alone in the airplane, I become a part of the machine and the process itself – it might as well be the reason why my photography feels like a constant strive to perfection. There is the technique, constant attention, analysis, and a lot of trial and error. Since my photography lives in a form of large format prints, detail is key. Way too many photographs have been lost to an imperfect focus or blur due to a slow shutter speed. Unfortunately I often learn about these mistakes after the fact – there is no time for in-depth review up there.

The Road Ends
Filip Wolak
Central New Jersey, 2016

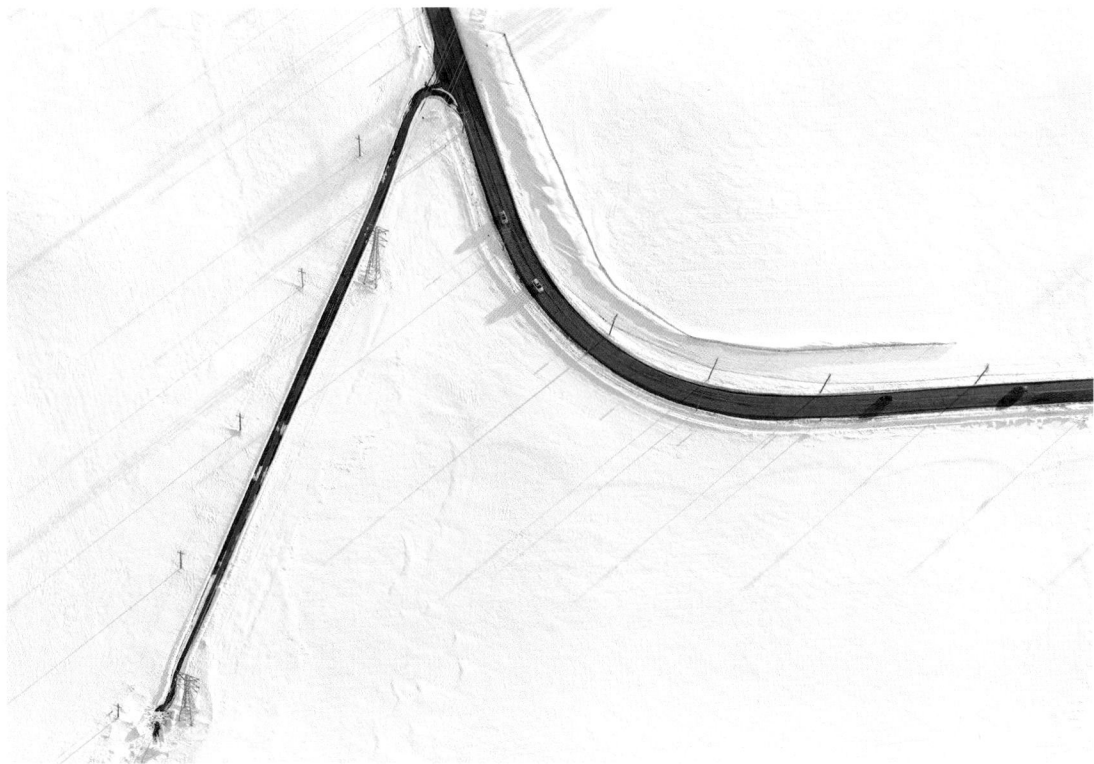

Everything needs to be planned well ahead and the pre-flight preparation is only a small part of the process. In the air, you will very rarely find yourself in an ideal position to shoot. Usually once the observation is made, I have to plan my approach wisely as many factors are then in play. The wind will almost always push you away from your original path, and if not corrected it will cause you to miss your intended frame. The perfect overhead position is one challenge, the shooting angle must also be carefully aligned because the angle at which the nose of the airplane is pointing will not necessarily be the one you would like for the frame to be. I try to slow down as much as possible, the slower the airplane flies, the greater the effect of the wind. But only at slow speeds it is possible to open the window comfortably – the speeds are still well above 60 mph (100 km/h).

Central Park from 10,000 Feet
Filip Wolak
New York City, 2016

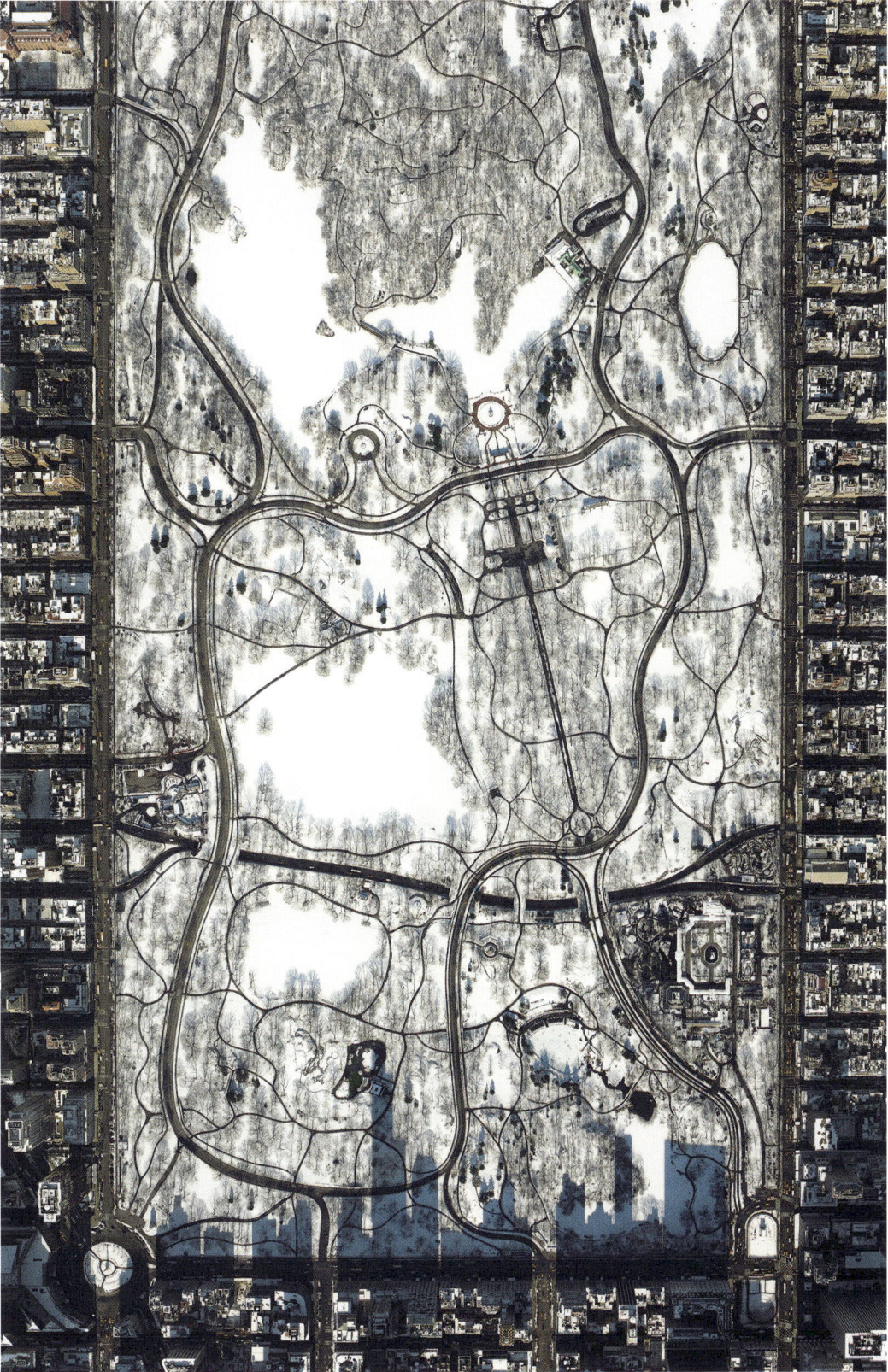

I usually photograph leaning out of the window, looking directly through a viewfinder, or I am holding the camera in my hands monitoring the screen. Gloves offer only short-term protection, and I wear goggles to protect the eyes from the wind. In the look-down perspective there is exactly enough space for a 50mm frame, anything wider will include the strut and the wheel. Holding the camera in my hands gives me an ultimate control over the final frame – there is still a little play for adjustments. Attempts to mount a camera on a wing strut for a wider view weren't very satisfying – I have found myself missing the shots more often than not. It was like having a camera mounted on a constantly moving tripod. It felt really disconnected (perhaps this is the reason why I do not use drones!) There's something wild in the act of sticking your head out of a moving airplane, and for as much as it is uncomfortable at the time, I would totally miss it if it was taken away from me.

Brooklyn
Filip Wolak
Brooklyn, New York, 2016

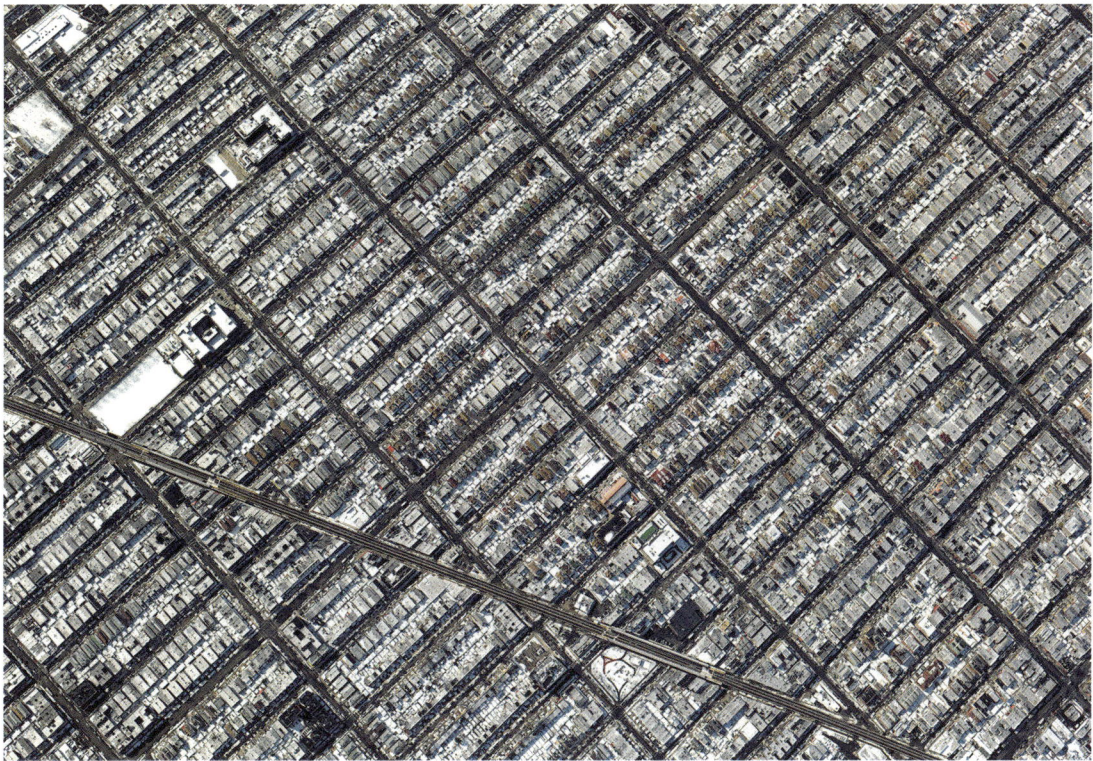

Flying the airplane safely while getting a technically perfect shot is only a part of the challenge. Approaching the chosen position, there are times when I cannot see the subject until the very last moment. There is a lot of "feeling" involved, almost like my third eye sees and aligns me properly in my turns. In my "Being Above" series, I take this to the next level by trying to position myself above an airliner that travels at 200 kts as I try to capture both the ground in context and the airplane above it. Changes of altitude are common, call it +/- 300 feet, but any such change alters your frame. I use primes almost exclusively for best quality. Flying over cities adds extra complexity of communication with a controller, and then even more precise flying is required. I always wear an in-ear headphone to monitor the channel and respond to requests when called. One day an air traffic controller reprimanded me with "stop taking photos," which immediately got my attention as I had missed his call. In such situations, or in the case of longer trips I do like the company of a pilot who actually flies the airplane and communicates with the ATC while I shoot freely. They not only need to be good aviators, they also need to have enormous patience with me!

Dense Forest
Filip Wolak
Around New York City, 2016

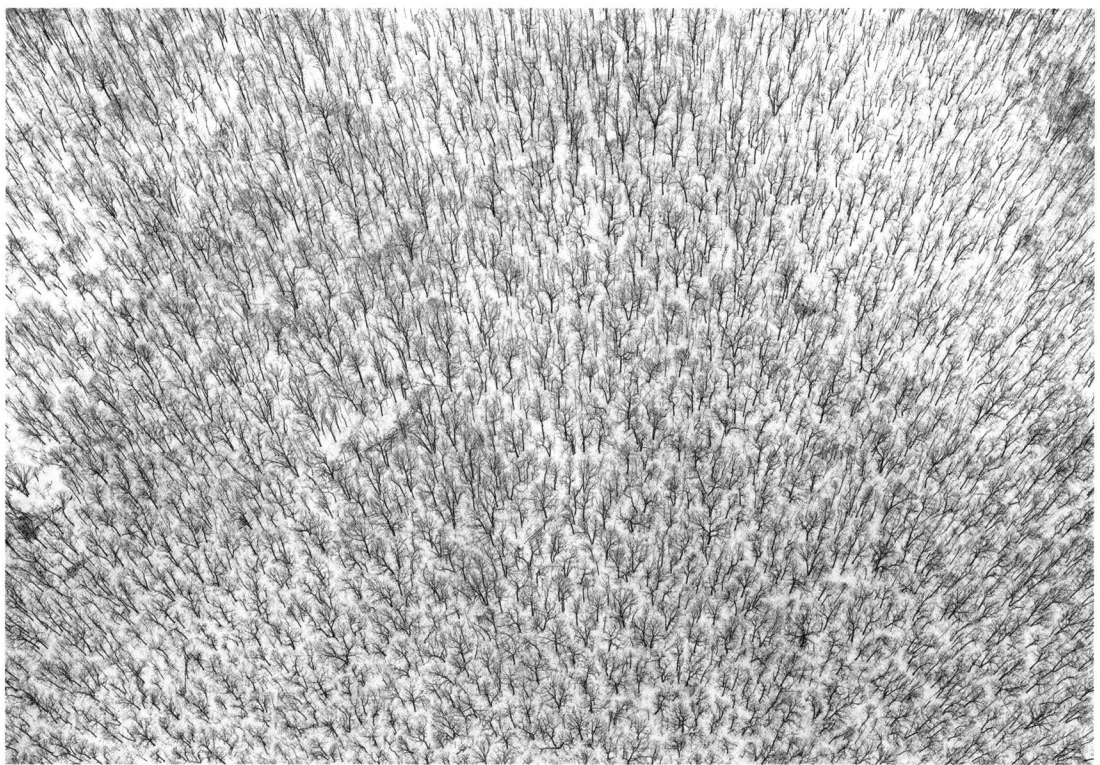

My work is best experienced in its original, large format. Usually printed
on a slightly textured paper that compliments the elements – I usually
choose different papers for different photographs, projects or "seasons."
Winter is usually printed on Hahnemuhle German Etching, anything
with sand or earth on an HM Perl or Baryta. My images do invite a
closer inspection so the texture is an important part of the piece. Color
correction (in anything but winter) is usually the main effort in post
production – hazy air usually introduces a lot of blue cast that needs to
be removed. Winter images are usually processed in black and white,
and then use the processed image as luma as I desaturate certain colors
appropriately (blues). For presentation, I prefer simple frames with no
glaze so that the viewer can almost "touch" the piece. Unframed pieces
also hold well, an elegant paper here is a sufficient medium for the story.

In my previous exhibitions, I have also shown select pieces in a top-down
view perspective, placing the print on a 4 foot high elevated platform. It is
an interesting experiment that brings the viewer closer to the moment that
I experienced while being in the skies – my ultimate goal after all, is to
share with you the beauty and magic of the moment of being above.

Lady Ice
Filip Wolak
Upstate New York, 2019

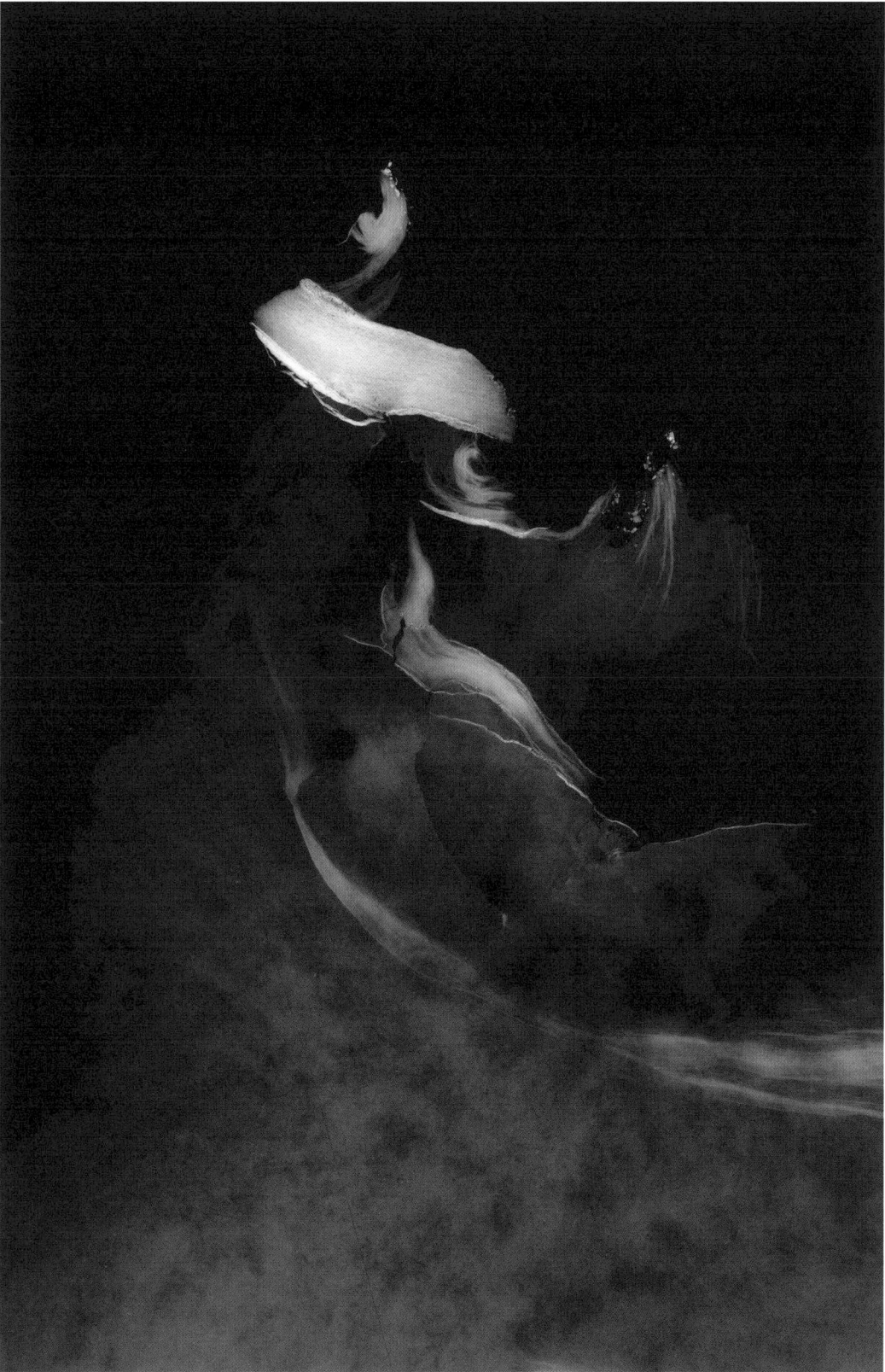

FILIP WOLAK

Filip Wolak is a professional photographer,
pilot and a flight instructor based in NYC. His
work has received many prestigious awards
and it has been published and exhibited in
several countries.

www.filipwolak.com

SUBURBIA/DISTURBIA

Ballarat, 2021

Ray Harris

The suburban aesthetic: individual,
sometimes eccentric, often
accidental. For some it is an attempt
to create order out of chaos,
for others chaos triumphs. This
modernist building sits in a back
lane in Ballarat, where the blank
wall is an open invitation to vandals.

Graffiti
Ray Harris
Central Ballarat, 2021

The Ballarat suburb of Wendouree (Aboriginal for "go away") is dotted with vacant lots and play parks for children. I cross this open space on my way to the local shops. This time the owner had decided to prune his hedge, leaving the branches exposed.

Exposed
Ray Harris
Wendouree, 2021

As summer approaches, the citizens of Ballarat pull down their sun blinds against the searing Australian heat. Who knows why the owner planted this one solitary plant?

Lonely
Ray Harris
Wendouree, 2021

I returned to this street to photograph something else. I turned and saw this. The plants seemed to be straining to escape.

Triffids
Ray Harris
Wendouree, 2021

Wendouree is a suburb in transition. The older houses are being replaced by the new. The symmetry of this facade was inescapable.

Symmetry
Ray Harris
Wendouree, 2021

This is very Australian, very 60s. Built on a slope, the builder placed the stairway of this brick veneer at the very front. It reminds me of a classical temple built on a hill.

Temple
Ray Harris
North Ballarat, 2021

Ballarat is a growth center. New suburbs
surround the old. The occasional bold
modernist statement punctuates the
otherwise bland sameness of the suburbs.

Six skies
Ray Harris
North Ballarat, 2021

RAY HARRIS

Ray Harris has retired. He now has plenty of
time to explore with his new camera.

THE EARLIEST LIGHT

England, Wales and Spain, 2021-2022

Kasra Karimi

The Great Orion Nebula (Messier 42) is known as the jewel of the night sky. This enormous cloud of gas and dust lies in the constellation of Orion, 1344 light years away from us.

I took this photo on the last day of 2021 with an equatorial tracking mount, an astronomy dedicated camera and a refractor telescope. Thanks to hours of exposure time, the dark skies of Cáceres province in Spain and also cutting edge technology that I am lucky to have access to, I was able to photograph The Orion Nebula.

The Great Orion Nebula
Kasra Karimi
Cáceres, Spain - December 31, 2021

The Cygnus Wall is a part of The North
America Nebula (NGC 7000) in the
constellation of Cygnus. This is a star-making
factory that is 2200 light years away from us.
The thick layer of dust and gas in the middle
that blocks a lot of stars behind it, resembles a
chalk sketch.

I took this photo in September 2021 over
several nights as I couldn't gather enough data
due to bad weather.

The Cygnus Wall
Kasra Karimi
Buckinghamshire, England - September, 2021

Wanting to photograph The Rosette Nebula (NGC 2244) encouraged me to learn astrophotography in the first place. I clearly remember the moment I first saw a photo of this nebula taken with a Canon 6D camera at The Astronomy Photography of the Year event held at the National Maritime Museum in Greenwich, London.

In the constellation of Monoceros, this nebula is 5200 light years away from us.

Although this photo was taken with a one-shot colour camera, I tried to replicate the Hubble Palette colour scheme to produce a colourful image.

The Rosette Nebula
Kasra Karimi
Cáceres, Spain - December 31, 2021

This photo benefits from 6 hours of exposure time. The Triangulum Galaxy (Messier 33) is 2.7 million light years away from us. I drove 3 hours to Halesworth in Suffolk, England, camped and took this picture in October 2021.

For deep space targets that emit light in a broad spectrum – like galaxies and reflection nebulae – having access to dark skies with minimum light pollution is a huge advantage. I also made sure that I took this photo during the new moon, when the night sky wasn't lit by the moonlight.

The Triangulum Galaxy
Kasra Karimi
Suffolk, England - October, 2021

The Flaming Star Nebula (IC 405) in the
constellation Auriga is 1500 light years away
from us. I took this photo during a cold
winter night for over 6 hours until it went
behind a tall tree. After that, we experienced
two weeks of extreme storms in the UK,
which was a perfect opportunity for me to
stay in, process and edit this photo. This is an
emission as well as a reflection nebula.

The Flaming Star Nebula
Kasra Karimi
Suffolk, England - February, 2022

The Ghost of Cassiopeia (IC 63) incidentally is high up in our night sky around Halloween. Located 550 light years away in the constellation of Cassiopeia, this emission nebula is simply hydrogen that is being bombarded with ultraviolet radiation from the nearby star Gamma Cassiopeiae.

This is the second time that I photographed IC 63 and this time I was able to improve my skills and photograph a nebula that was an honorary mention by NASA's Astronomy Photo of the Day.

The Ghost of Cassiopeia
Kasra Karimi
Suffolk, England - October, 2021

Barnard 33 (aka The Horsehead Nebula)
is 1500 light years away from us and lies in
the constellation of Orion. I find this target
particularly challenging to photograph because
of the two very bright stars that are close
to the Horsehead, which is quite dim. Very
bright stars, like Alnitak, cause star halos in my
optical system. Having the halos under control
has certainly proved to be challenging.

The Horsehead Nebula
Kasra Karimi
Suffolk, England - February, 2022

KASRA KARIMI

Kasra Karimi is an Iranian-British artist and
filmmaker based in London. Filmmaking is his
passion, but in 2018 Karimi dived into the world
of astrophotography.

www.kasrakarimi.co.uk

THOSE MAGICAL MOMENTS

An interview with photographer **Donald Miralle**

By W. Scott Olsen

"Sports photography is its own kind of art," he says. "It's genre photography. And if it's done at the highest level, it's very artistic. It's all in the way you approach it. There are some amazing sports photographers I consider artists. I consider myself an artist as well."

I am talking with Donald Miralle, who holds more than 50 international awards, including six World Press Awards, seven Pictures of the Year International Sports Photographer of the Year Awards, NPPA Best of Photojournalism Awards, an Emmy nomination, CLIO award and more.

"There are different ways to approach sports photography," he says. "If you're going to a live event, and you're documenting that event, say you're working for one of the agencies, then you're just freezing moments in time. Reporting. But if you're approaching it to put your visual stamp on it, your style or way of seeing things, you take an artistic view."

People say you're innovative, that you see things other people don't.
"There are moments, whether it's sports or news, whether it's Robert Capa or Walter Iooss Jr., where they're freezing these amazing

moments. I think it crosses over to art when it's not only an amazing moment, but the photographer, the way he sees it, the way he decides to present it in that medium, is an art portrayal. You know that person's style. You see their stamp on it. For me, I feel like my style is graphic. I like shooting using leading lines or leading colors, or even if it's black and white composition, using that dark and white in there. It comes down to like art school when I was a kid. It's just seeing it your way when you're given

an assignment. You have to see it your way. That's who you are."

"I feel like the same elements – composition, color, the graphic aspect of using lines and rules of thirds, and how are you using this canvas to display something, and how the viewer's eye views that canvas and moves around in it, and how it's revealed – that interpretation is what makes it art."

You tell me you're drawn to the edges, drawn to sports, drawn to adventuring. Tell me about the little kid in the backyard, jumping off the fence?
"The little kid jumping off the fence in the backyard got hurt a lot. Pushing it and pushing

it hard, coming home with skinned knees and having to explain stuff to my parents. I grew up always outside and athletic. But I really didn't pick up photography till later in my young adult life. When I was younger, I was always drawing and painting. I was that kid who drew in high school yearbooks. When I went to UCLA, I was a biology major, thinking pre-med, and I was on the swim team. But what I enjoyed most was always more arts than science, even though I felt like there is a weird correlation between art and science. When I took my first elective, photography, it literally clicked. It was the same principles that work for other fine art mediums. I wasn't bending over a canvas with oil paint all over my hands, and I wasn't sculpting something in clay, but I was still freezing time. And from that point on, I was hooked on photography."

"My dad saw this ad in the LA Times for photographers, editors, librarians for this sports photography agency called Allsport. I had no idea they were the biggest sport agency in the world at the time. When I walked into my interview, I was just this green kid, just out of college. I brought in my college portfolio, which was pictures of my friends. The guy looked at it and said yeah, mate, you're pretty inexperienced with photography. I can't offer you the photography job, but I can offer you a job at the picture desk, right over there."

It was 1997, leading up to the 1998 Nagano Olympics. I was there every night and the photos being fed to me were from the Olympics. My baptism by fire for sports

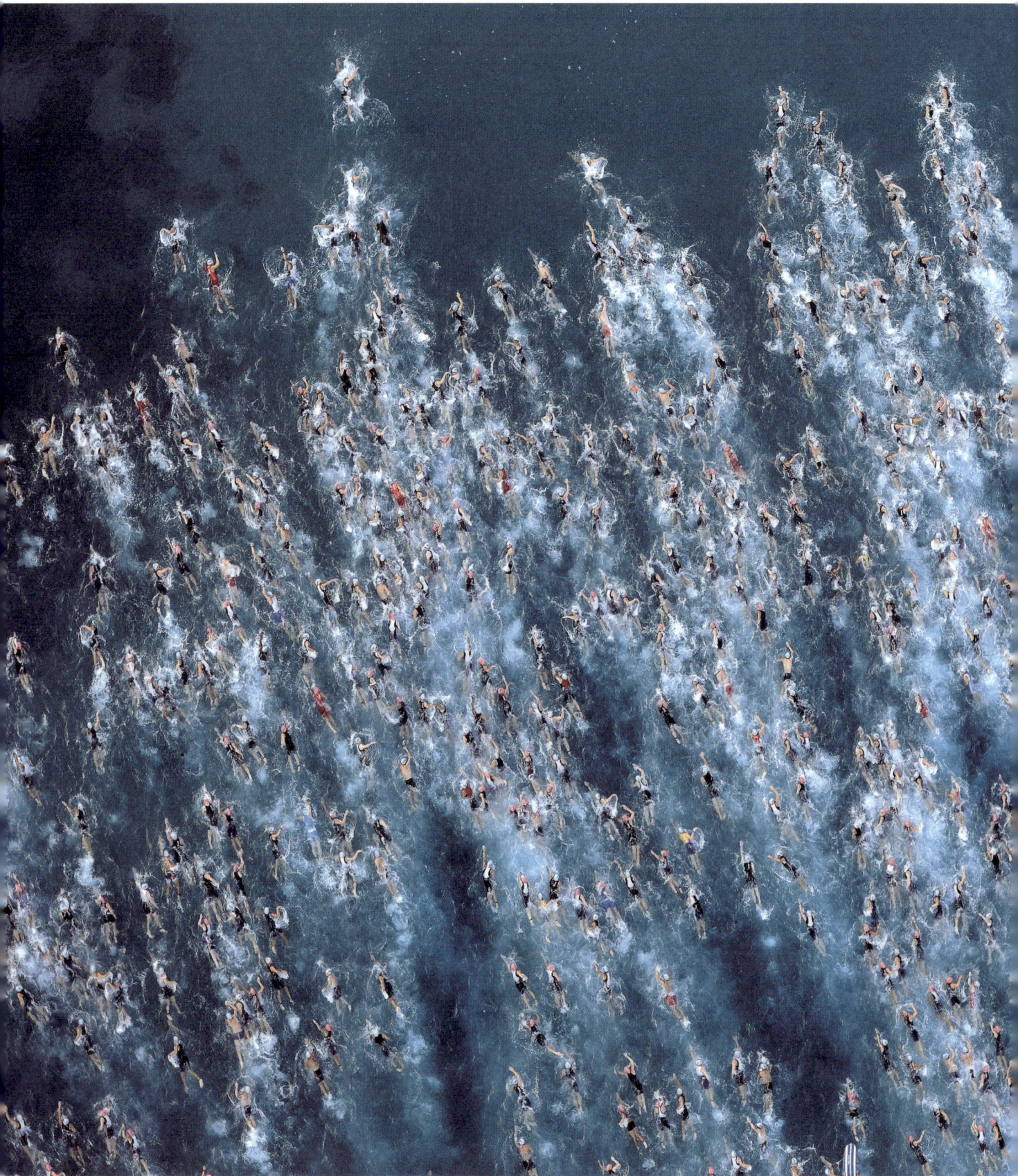

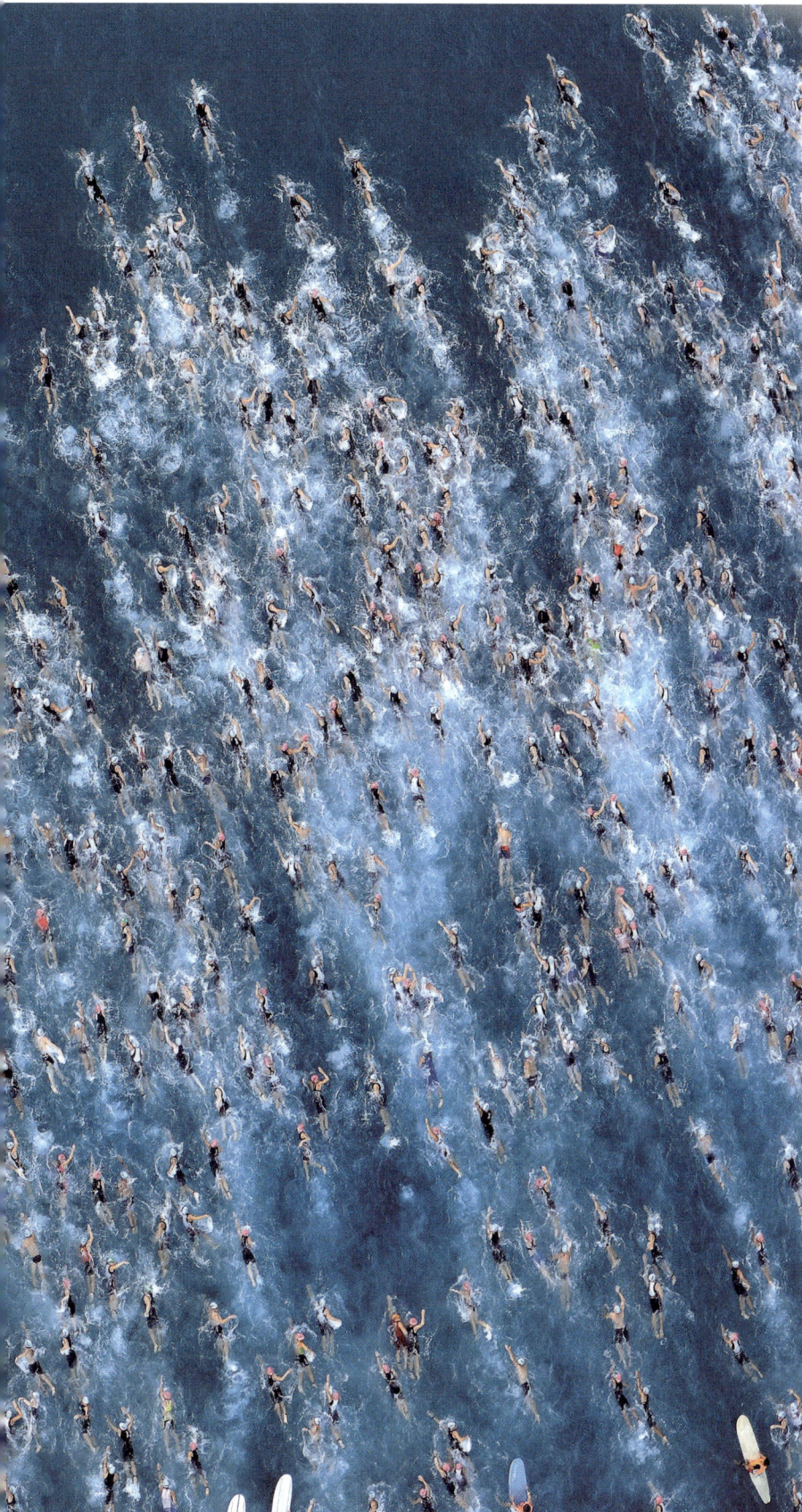

photography was seeing the Olympic games come over, going Wow, this photography is amazing. I would get these scanned photos, have to clean them up, have to caption them, and then send them out to all the AP wires. It was kind of fortuitous. I learned all the facets of photography. I learned the business side where you have account executives putting in requests for photos from different agencies or publications, and I learned the refiling side. Then I learned the technical side of the photographers in the field, which is where I wanted to be. I learned all these different pieces and then a year later, I ended up being the Photographer of the Year for Allsport."

"Ten years later, I left and for 15 years now I've been a freelancer."

Until you've got decades of experience, how do you approach composition at any live sport? Are your decisions experience based? Are you looking for something specific?

"I think this has to do a lot with me being an athlete and knowing the nuances of sport. You're looking for these little nuances and trying to capture them. A lot of people don't notice these things, like the way water is going to bead off of a swimmer's back a certain way, or watching a football game and knowing that something's going to happen, and being able to predict it and putting yourself in a position where you're capturing the cleanest moment. It comes down to proper preparation. You need to get yourself in a position with your gear, to give you the highest chance of not only a good moment, but a clean, great moment."

"Preparation is going into a live event where you have no control and improvising with the environment that's given to you. You're thrown into a situation where you have to quickly be on top of what's happening and on the top your toes with your gear. You have to realize what's happening, and where it might happen next. You have to be aware of what you're dealing with lighting wise and background wise. But the other side is if it's not a live event, and it's a controlled environment, like a commercial shoot where we have full control over everything. You get to control the lighting; you've controlled the background. You could have an art director telling you they need something for their brand. Or maybe they say we want the portrait of this

athlete to look like this. But then things unfold, and as things are unfolding, whether it's a portrait or live action, or a commercial, you have to be able to improvise and be able to be fluid with that change. You go into every shoot with an idea of how you think it is going to happen. This is going to be the best shot. This is the shot I'm envisioning going in there. Nine times out of ten, though, that's not the best shot. It kind of unfolds and then next thing you know, you have something that is way better because it's not what you expected."

Tell me a picture that just was magic for you?
"I was in Tokyo, at the Olympics, and I took this picture of Caleb Dressel breaking out of the water. One of those little nuance moments that I knew, because two years before, and I was at the World Championships, trying to get this photo of him bursting out of the water. I kind of knew what it looked like when the water came off him for a second, but when I did it in South Korea, I had one chance to do it

and I didn't nail it. I didn't get it exactly how I wanted. I don't know whether it was the angle, the shutter speed, or maybe the focus wasn't tack on. And when I did it again in Tokyo, I feel like I got it. I nailed that picture. And when you feel like you nail a picture and you get it as good as you can get it, then that's something you can be proud of."

"Then again, I was taking pictures yesterday at the beach. I took a picture at my little surf spot. I was up on the cliff and I shot a guy coming through this little barrel that was backlit. It was lit up all green. It was a beautiful little moment. Day to day, I try to use photography. I make a visual log. I mean, that's what I put on social media. My Instagram is what I see during the day. And when I see a magical moment. I just think: you know, you're only as good as your last picture. That's my last picture I took yesterday."

DEPTH AND SPEED:
INSIDE GETTY IMAGES SPORTS

An interview with **Maxx Wolfson**,
Director of Sports Photography for the Americas

by W. Scott Olsen

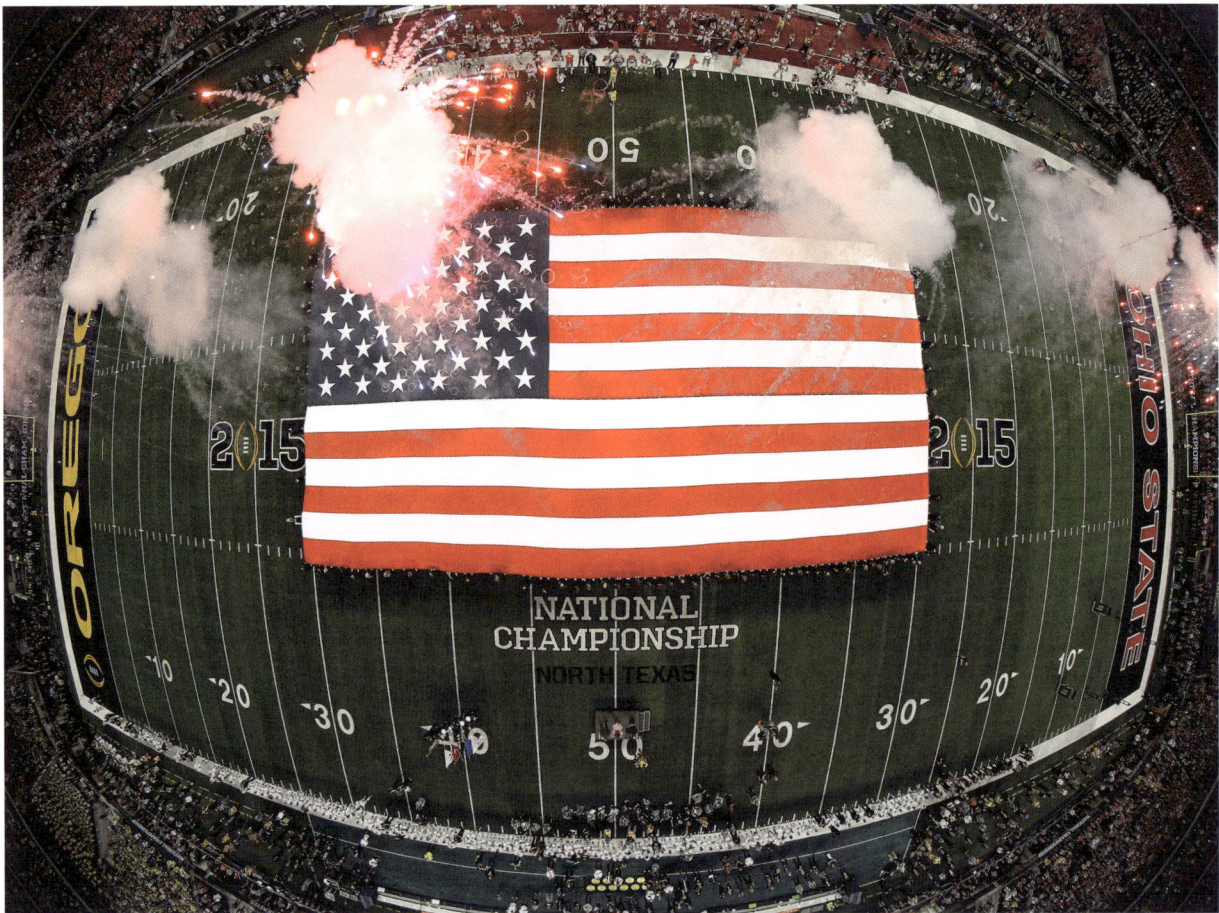

© Photo Tom Pennington/Getty Images

Imagine the thrill and the responsibility. The Superbowl and the Olympics. World Cup competitions. Sailing and tennis and curling, too. The world will see these events through your lens. There is a need to be both comprehensive as well as selective. There is a monumental need for speed.

Getty Images is ubiquitous. Their photographers all over the world are charged with bringing the news of competition – insightfully and immediately.

Maxx Wolfson has been working for Getty Images for more than nineteen years. Beginning in 2003 as a Field Editor, since 2018 he has been Director of Sports Photography. Images from every major sporting event in the Americas as well as around the world cross his desk. He directs a team of talented photographers and support staff whose goal is the capture the fleeting and ineffable emotions of sport, and then make sure the world can see them.

"Our photographers have experience as well as knowledge," he tells me. "Our photographers pride themselves on their knowledge. In football, for example, they know there's a new

rookie who's going to play left tackle. They know a veteran's habits. So, when it does come down to that end of game moment, they're in the right position, and they might be doing something different than the rest of the people who don't do the preparation work."

"For Super Bowls, we have to look out for the offense, the defense, coaches, fans, celebrities and really all parts of the game, because we have such a large customer base. We don't know who is going to end up with these images, so we're shooting all of it. We have a strategy in terms of positioning on the field, to get a quarterback's reaction, which is something that is always used. And we want the key action picture of an actual touchdown catch."

Do shooters get to do much selecting?
"It's something that has changed and evolved since I started as an editor. When I was editing, we would see every single picture shot by the photographer. Now with technology, we're able to have the photographers tag pictures in camera. And the images are essentially beamed

National Championship - Oregon v Ohio State

ARLINGTON, TX - JANUARY 12: A view of the American flag during the national anthem performed by Lady Antebellum prior to the College Football Playoff National Championship Game between the Oregon Ducks and the Ohio State Buckeyes at AT&T Stadium on January 12, 2015 in Arlington, Texas.

© Photo Jamie Squire/Getty Images

Above

AFC Divisional Playoffs - Buffalo Bills v Kansas City Chiefs

KANSAS CITY, MISSOURI - JANUARY 23: Tyreek Hill #10 of the Kansas City Chiefs scores a 64 yard touchdown against the Buffalo Bills during the fourth quarter in the AFC Divisional Playoff game at Arrowhead Stadium on January 23, 2022 in Kansas City, Missouri.

to an editor. The editor is moving as quickly as possible, getting that image out sometimes in as little as 30 seconds.

"Viral moments happen all the time. For example, when Tyreek Hill put up the peace sign against the Buffalo Bills on his way to the end zone during the AFC Divisional Round. You can't plan for viral moments, but they are always fun to capture and that's when our Sales team really goes to work."

Talk to me about preparation, both at your level and at the shooter's level?

"The preparation for our photographers actually begins with our Operations Team. For us, for example, preparation for the Olympics begins the day a country is awarded the games. For this last one, Beijing started in 2015. Funny enough,

we were in Beijing in 2008, so we had a good knowledge of the city and the area. Obviously, we didn't do much in the mountains back in 2008, since it was the summer games, but we knew the venues and we knew where the media center was going to be. That definitely helped, rather than going into a city completely blind. But we have a very experienced Operations Team whose job focuses strictly on preparations for Olympic Games, World Cups and other major sporting events."

Do they scout sites, get permissions? Handle logistics? More?

"Yes, they're scouting sites which is all part of the planning process. They're a part of the background. They'll look at the venues and say, 'you know, a camera here with this background, would look great. Let's see what we can do to get that.' And they also do technical trips. Our technical team will travel multiple times to the Olympic city and do test events. They think about if we need cables in various spots throughout the venues, so our photographers can plug indirectly to a line and send back to our editors in the Main Media Center and to remote editors across the globe. The team spends a lot of time in catwalks looking for different angles and they work with the Organizing Committee to see what the field of play will look like.

Individual shots are not the photographer's idea?

"They are the photographer's idea. And in the sense that the photographers are the ones scouting those locations ahead of and during the Games each day to find the best or new, creative angles. But with use of remote camera

© Photo Tom Pennington/Getty Images

Left

Alpine Skiing - Beijing 2022 Winter Olympics Day 0

YANQING, CHINA - FEBRUARY 04: Matteo Marsaglia of Team Italy skis during the Men's Downhill 2nd training session ahead of the Beijing 2022 Winter Olympic Games at National Alpine Ski Centre on February 04, 2022 in Yanqing, China.

technology, especially in the catwalks of venues, there are so many people involved to get that shot. Whether it's the technology to beam it back within seconds, the photographer who does the tour to set up them up, the technician who's actually sitting there and tightening the screws to make sure that camera is safely secured, or the editor who will ultimately decide which image to send. With remote cameras, there's a photographer actually hitting the button to get the shot, with their name that gets put on the picture, but everybody knows it's a team effort, and its very cool when it all comes together.

What type of preparation do your photographers usually have before they cover an event?

"They do their homework. We do a lot of work for the US Olympic team, as well as the Canadian Olympic team and for Team Great Britain and Australia, to name a few. So, we're always looking out for our different customers. But we're also looking to tell the story of the games, whether it's a small country that might not be on the radar, but for some reason might have the best team in the world for a specific sport. We expect our photographers to do that homework. They're also getting shot lists and getting prepped by our Operations team. They get an email the night before an event, saying they need to be at the venue at this time, here are the 20 athletes you need to look out for, and so on. That same list is going to our editors as well. The photographer and editor work together, in constant communication throughout, texting each other going, "Hey, nice picture of 'Joe Smith'. However, can you get another one from the back?"

"That conversation is constantly happening as our editors watch the event, either on a closed circuit TV, or back on the NBC app, whatever it might be. And sometimes they hear what the broadcasters say and notice they're talking a lot about this move or that technique, whatever it might be, and we can get a shot of that immediately."

So you have real time art direction going on during sporting events?

"Absolutely, for the Olympics and Super Bowl, as well as other major sporting events. We use rehearsals as a way to scout locations to get an idea of where to look and who to cover. For the Super Bowl, we have radios. I'm talking to the photographers the entire time and they're talking to me the entire time. However, I ultimately trust the photographers to make their own decisions when it gets to that crucial moment of the game. I know that they know where to be, but there are lots of other things going on too. Like, 'Hey, Jay Z is sitting in one of the suites, go take picture of him.' We're always trying to be the larger eyes and ears for our photographers as they focus on the field."

Right

Ice Hockey - Beijing 2022 Winter Olympics Day 6

BEIJING, CHINA - FEBRUARY 10: Shimisi Jieruimi #45 of Team China misses the puck in the second period of the game against Team United States during the Men's Ice Hockey Preliminary Round Group A match on Day 6 of the Beijing 2022 Winter Olympic Games at National Indoor Stadium on February 10, 2022 in Beijing, China.

*Super Bowl XLVII -
Baltimore Ravens v San
Francisco 49ers*

NEW ORLEANS,
LA - FEBRUARY 03:
A general view of
the Mercedes-Benz
Superdome after
a sudden power
outage that lasted
34 minutes in the
second half during
Super Bowl XLVII
between the Baltimore
Ravens and the San
Francisco 49ers at
the Mercedes-Benz
Superdome on
February 3, 2013
in New Orleans,
Louisiana.

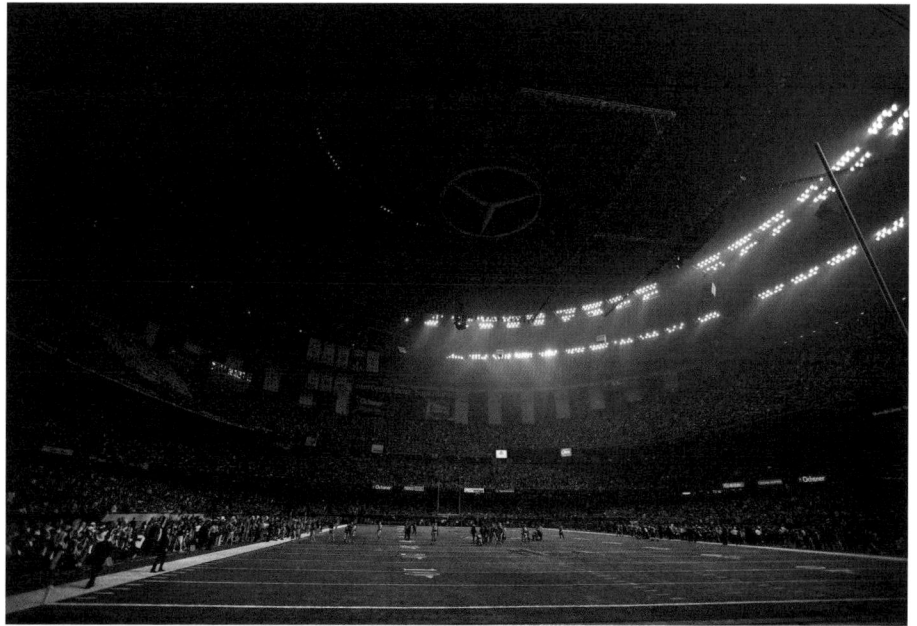

© Photo Al Bello/Getty Images

"I'm also always checking Twitter. I'm seeing what just went viral. Sometimes an idea pops up on Twitter and I relay that to the photographers and now we have an image of it."

Your photographers shooting something in the Olympics like the Downhill or Super G have actually skied into their positions. Those are not easy slopes.

"Oh, yeah, absolutely. And their photography kit that day is their cameras, their lenses, their skis, and everything else they need for the day. We need photographers who can actually ski with 60 pounds of gear on their back for these instances."

"It's not for everybody. Our two Alpine specialists have been to five or six events already this winter, in preparation of the Winter Olympics, to make sure they're physically able to do it. And there's also the mental part of sitting on the side of a mountain. Sometimes you just sit there for hours and it's freezing cold. You have to be prepared, with winter gear and the right attitude."

"We do pride ourselves in having the best photographers in the world. And we do have a range of specialists for certain sports. Not everybody's a winter sports specialist, but they're still amazing photographers. And sometimes what excites me more is putting somebody who's an incredible photographer to shoot something they might not shoot every day,

and seeing what they see, which is typically something different."

Given the need for getting images out quickly, is there any time for post-production tweaking?

"When editing, we're finding the picture within the picture. We're not doing anything in terms of photoshop skills, or tricks, or any of that. I've done this for so many years and I don't want to learn that and have never wanted to learn it. Cropping for impact is something we do, and we might do a very light touch up in terms of the color, but it's very, very minimal. We try to get our pictures out as quickly as possible and are held to high editorial standards when it comes to any post-production work."

Have you ever timed how fast, from shutter release to making it available to your customers?

"I've had multiple Olympics where I've had somebody sitting over my shoulder with a stopwatch trying to time it. We got it down to under 30 seconds at the Tokyo Olympics and now in Beijing -- from the time the shutter is pressed to when the image hits my computer, I do a quick Photoshop, caption it, and push it out. This is incredible compared to where it used to be. And the crazy thing is our competitors know that. They try to get faster and faster, too. But we're still the fastest. It's a fun competition, but now it's also something now our customers expect."

Above

*Ice Hockey - Beijing
2022 Winter Olympics
Day 2*

BEIJING, CHINA -
FEBRUARY 06: Team
United States huddle
up prior to the start of
the game against Team
Switzerland during the
Women's Preliminary
Round Group A
match at Wukesong
Sports Center on
February 06, 2022 in
Beijing, China.

Is there an image that you, as editor, are particularly proud of?

"From day one, I wanted to get into the video board at AT&T Stadium in Arlington, Texas. I just knew it would be an incredible picture, overlooking the whole field, shooting straight down. We worked for years to get in there. And then for the college football championship in 2015, we finally got permission. We worked with media relations, people within the stadium, the organizing committee from the college football playoff. It was the first time they'd ever had a camera up there. It just really worked out."

"I think a lot of people don't understand our vision at times. Sometimes we see things they don't see. We try to explain it the right way. But at AT&T, for example, there's this tiny little one or two person elevator and you're lifted hundreds of feet up into the air to hang a camera above the playing field. It scared a lot of people. But I explained, we know how to do it the right way. I wasn't worried about that."

"We put it up a few days before the game. We just kind of prayed everything worked. And all of a sudden, a giant American flag covered the whole field and there were fireworks going off. It's an amazing image to this day. We ended up seeing it used everywhere, which is great. And we gave copies of that to the staff who helped us get up the elevator because we thought they were such a big part of making that picture."

Was there ever an event where everything went wrong, no matter how much preparation and talent were available?

"Oh, man, this is an easy one. We were at Super Bowl XLVII in New Orleans and the power went out. Beyonce was performing the halftime show and pictures were flying out. Everything was great, everything was golden. All of a sudden, boom, the power goes out between the end of halftime and the start of the third quarter. We had a bunch of servers; we had our whole tech team there and essentially, we had to put every single picture onto my laptop and use my cell phone to get pictures out. It was intense to say the least."

Talk to me about quality. From your editor's chair to a shooter on some field, what does quality mean?

"Quality is everything. I've killed so many pictures over the years because the quality wasn't there. We pride ourselves on not only being in the best position, with the best timing, but having the best background. As an editor, my name isn't on the picture. But the photographer's name is on the photo, and I did everything I could to make that picture the highest quality image possible. Every single Monday morning we have a call going over our best sports pictures from that week. We are our toughest critics. If there's something wrong, as simple as a trashcan in the frame, we don't use it.

RESHAPING REALITY

Lynne Blount

Reshaping Reality

"The world of reality has its limits; the world of imagination is boundless."
— Jean-Jacques Rousseau

I use my camera as a paintbrush with the intention of transforming the familiar into something new. In the last few years, I have become almost obsessed with colours, shapes, and textures, wherever they may be hiding. I have always found genre labels limiting, as they imply a boundary to what might be possible in both technique and output and for that reason I prefer to use "experimental" as the main descriptor of my work.

"The world is but a canvas to our imagination." — *Henry David Thoreau*

I enjoy making ephemeral images, the kind of images our brains store as a memory. I want to convey how I feel about a place or an object as well as provide something unique for the viewer to ponder. Seeking out the "essence" rather than the reality, I often half close my eyes to see the picture I want to create. Much of my work is inspired by the natural world around me. I can be mesmerized by a fast-flowing river; the reeds as they billow in the wind, or by very mundane objects in my house and neighbourhood. I enjoy sculpture, especially the work of Henry Moore and, with the permission of the Henry Moore Foundation in 2018, I began a project with a friend to re-imagine his work.

To make my images I use three main techniques: "In the Round," Intentional Camera Movement (ICM) and Multiple Exposures (MEs).

Made famous by Pep Ventosa, images made using the "In the Round" technique require time-consuming post processing. Having made up to fifty images by walking around the subject, I use the RAW converter in Lightroom to process each image individually, before transferring them as layers into Photoshop. Working from the second layer from the bottom, I reduce the opacity of each layer by five or ten percent, as I move up the stack. The layers are blended with a variety of blend modes and distractions are masked out.

"When you are experimenting you have to try so many things before you choose what you want, you may go days getting nothing but exhaustion."
— Fred Astaire

My aim is always to make the picture I want in-camera, however, there is an element of serendipity in both ICM and ME techniques which may necessitate layering images further in Photoshop. I may combine two ICM images or MEs or an ME with an ICM. I may also use the RAW converter to process the same image in two or more different ways, before combining them in Photoshop.

When experimenting with ICM, I move my camera around in different directions until I capture something interesting. I study each failed image to ascertain the time I need to spend on a particular area to create more detail or a different effect. On a good day, I may achieve three images out of one hundred that I like.

"I found I could say things with colour that I couldn't say in any other way — things that I had no words for." — *Georgia O'Keefe*

I am often asked what settings I used to create a particular ME. The truth is, I have no idea. The camera does not record which part of the Kelvin scale I selected or the blend mode I chose for each image and my brain cannot retain such information. There is no set process when creating an in-camera ME, other than focussing on the same subject whilst experimenting with the settings. The colours achieved depend on the quality of the light at the time, the colour of the subject, the white balance and blend mode chosen, and of course how I process the image in Lightroom or Photoshop.

Whilst these demanding techniques ensure the final image is totally unique, I can never go back to improve a particular photograph as there are just too many variables at play.

"I think it's important to remember that making art is a process. It is never finished. The occupation itself is one of process, exploration, and experimentation. It is one of questioning and examining." — *Mel Robson*

Autumn Red
Lynne Blount
Audley End, 2018

Golden Hues / Reproduced here, with the kind permission of the Henry Moore Foundation
Lynne Blount
Henry Moore Foundation, 2019

Seascape / Reproduced here, with the kind permission of the Henry Moore Foundation
Lynne Blount
Henry Moore Foundation, 2018

Framed
Lynne Blount
Essex, 2020

Peeling Triangles
Lynne Blount
Taken indoors, 2020

Sunlit Reeds
Lynne Blount
Wicken Fen, 2019

River Dance
Lynne Blount
Scotland, 2020

LYNNE BLOUNT

Lynne uses her camera as a paint brush to re-interpret the colours, shapes and textures around her. The images are created using mainly in-camera techniques such as multiple exposures and intentional camera movement. Lynne's photographs have won international awards and have been exhibited in Switzerland, London, and Birmingham.

www.lynneblount.com

FRAMES ONLINE

Get access to additional digital content including photography
masterclasses, in-depth photo analyses, insightful articles,
and private photography community forums.

Become a FRAMES Member for only $14 US per month
Shipping and handling of printed editions is already included in your membership fee.

readframes.com/join

CONTEXT

PHOTOGRAPHERS

John Paul Caponigro

Page 9 Canon EOS 5DS R + Canon EF 24-70mm F2.8 IS USM **Page 11** Canon EOS 5DS R + Canon EF 24-70mm F2.8 IS USM **Page 13** Canon EOS 5DS R + Canon EF 24-70mm F2.8 IS USM **Page 15** Canon EOS 5DS R + Canon EF 24-70mm F2.8 IS USM **Page 17** Canon EOS 5DS R + Canon EF 24-70mm F2.8 IS USM **Page 19** Canon EOS 5DS R + Canon EF 24-70mm F2.8 IS USM **Page 21** Canon EOS 5DS R + Canon EF 24-70mm F2.8 IS USM

Gary Beeber

Page 25 SONY Alpha 6 **Page 27** SONY Alpha 7 **Page 29** SONY Alpha 6 **Page 31** SONY Alpha 6 **Page 33** SONY Alpha 6 **Page 35** SONY Alpha 6 **Page 37** SONY Alpha 6

Filip Wolak

Page 41 Nikon D810 + 70-200 2.8GII **Pages 43 - 49** Nikon D810 + 50mm **Page 51** Nikon D810, 14-24mm **Page 53** Nikon D850 + Sigma 50mm

Ray Harris

Pages 57 - 63 Sony Alpha 7iii, Lightroom **Pages 65 - 69** Nikon D5600, Lightroom

Kasra Karimi

Pages 73 – 85 Telescope: TS-Optics 130 APO Triplet Refractor, **Camera:** ZWO ASI6200MC Pro, **Tracking Mount:** Skywatcher EQ6-R Pro, **Processing Software:** PixInsight and Adobe Photoshop

BEYOND

Lynne Blount

Page 101 Canon 5D Mark III 'In the Round' technique **Page 102** Canon 5D Mark III Multiple Exposures combined in-camera and re-combined Photoshop **Page 103** Olympus OMD EM1 MK II 60mm Macro Lens Multiple Exposures and ICM combined in-camera and recombined in Photoshop **Page 104** Canon EOS R In-camera multiple exposure. RAW processed in Lightroom only **Page 105** Canon EOS R In-camera multiple exposures re-combined in Photoshop **Page 106** Canon EOS R single ICM RAW processed only **Page 107** Canon EOS R Two ICMs combined in Photoshop